CHANGING SEASONS

17 Embroideries
to Mix and Match

GAIL PAN

Martingale
Create with Confidence

Changing Seasons: 17 Embroideries to Mix and Match
© 2019 by Gail Pan

Martingale®
19021 120th Ave. NE, Ste. 102
Bothell, WA 98011-9511 USA
ShopMartingale.com

MISSION STATEMENT

We empower makers who use fabric and yarn
to make life more enjoyable.

CREDITS

**PUBLISHER AND
CHIEF VISIONARY OFFICER**
Jennifer Erbe Keltner

CONTENT DIRECTOR	DESIGN MANAGER
Karen Costello Soltys	Adrienne Smitke
MANAGING EDITOR	**COVER AND INTERIOR DESIGNER**
Tina Cook	Regina Girard
TECHNICAL EDITOR	**PHOTOGRAPHER**
Carolyn Beam	Brent Kane
COPY EDITOR	**ILLUSTRATOR**
Kathleen Cubley	Sandy Loi

SPECIAL THANKS
*Photography for this book was taken at the
home of Julie Smiley of Des Moines, Iowa.*

Printed in China
24 23 22 21 20 19   8 7 6 5 4 3 2 1

**Library of Congress Cataloging-in-Publication Data is
available upon request.**

ISBN: 978-1-60468-993-8

Contents

INTRODUCTION

I am an embroiderer and a quilter from Australia who loves stitching! Whether spending time with friends or at home on the couch, I enjoy bringing fabric and thread together. Inspiration comes in many forms. While I'm out and about walking, shopping, or lunching with friends, things catch my eye, spurring ideas for embroidery designs.

The projects in this book are based around the changing days of our lives. Some of the quilts have interchangeable embroidery panels, making it easy to replace one embroidered piece with another. Sewing a decorative piece with interchangeable panels is especially helpful for those with limited quilting time, because just one quilt can display several embroidery options! Or you can make a quilt and use only a single embroidery panel. For example, the Our Home quilt (page 17) could easily have one embroidered saying sewn in place.

Use Celebration Banners (page 28) to decorate for a particular special event, then simply change one out as you move on to the next happy occasion. The What Makes You Happy banner (page 29) is great for the in-between times.

If you're an experienced embroiderer, you can jump right into the projects. If you need a bit more information about embroidery, you'll find what you need in "General Instructions" on page 60. Whatever your experience level, enjoy making the projects in the book and have fun on your stitching journey!

~ Gail

As the Seasons Change

As one season changes to the next, transform your home with interchangeable designs that reflect the best that each season has to offer.

× MATERIALS ×

Supplies are for one background quilt and four interchangeable embroidered panels. Yardage is based on 42"-wide fabric. Fat quarters measure 18" × 21".

½ yard of off-white print for embroidery backgrounds

¾ yard of lightweight fusible interfacing, 18" to 20" wide, for embroidery backing

1 fat quarter of cream print for quilt center

12 assorted print 2½"-wide strips of varying lengths for borders (see "Cutting" at right)

⅛ yard *each* of red, pumpkin, blue, and pink prints for embroidery bindings

⅓ yard of navy tone on tone for binding

4 rectangles, 7½" × 11", of backing fabric for embroideries

¾ yard of backing fabric

4 rectangles, 7½" × 11", of batting for embroideries

26" × 30" piece of batting

Pearl cotton, size 12, in four variegated colors for embroidery panels: pink (Spring), red (Summer), pumpkin (Autumn), navy (Winter)

Ecru pearl cotton, size 8, for hand quilting

5" x 18" strip of fabric for hanging sleeve (optional)

4 skirt hook-and-eye closures (hooks and bars), ⅝", for attaching the panels

Pigma pen for marking embroidery designs

× CUTTING ×

From the off-white print, cut:
- 1 strip, 13" × 42"; crosscut into 4 rectangles, 9" × 13"

From the lightweight fusible interfacing, cut:
- 2 strips, 13" × 20"; crosscut into 4 rectangles, 9" × 13"

From the cream print, cut:
- 1 rectangle, 9½" × 13½"

From the 12 assorted print strips, cut in the following order:*
- A: 1 strip, 2½" × 13½"
- B: 1 strip, 2½" × 11½"
- C: 1 strip, 2½" × 15½"
- D: 1 strip, 2½" × 13½"
- E: 1 strip, 2½" × 17½"
- F: 1 strip, 2½" × 15½"
- G: 1 strip, 2½" × 19½"
- H: 1 strip, 2½" × 17½"
- I: 1 strip, 2½" × 21½"
- J: 1 strip, 2½" × 19½"
- K: 1 strip, 2½" × 23½"
- L: 1 strip, 2½" × 21½"

From *each* of the embroidery binding fabrics, cut:
- 2 strips, 1½" × 42"

From the navy tone on tone, cut:
- 3 strips, 2½" × 42"

Label the strips and keep them in this order for sewing around the quilt center.

✕ EMBROIDERING THE DESIGNS ✕

1. Trace each of the spring, summer, autumn, and winter designs (pages 13–16) onto the right side of an off-white rectangle. Fuse an interfacing rectangle to the back of each marked rectangle.

2. Using one strand of pearl cotton, embroider the designs following the embroidery keys on the patterns.

3. Press the embroidery from the wrong side. Centering the embroidery, trim the rectangle to 7½" × 11½".

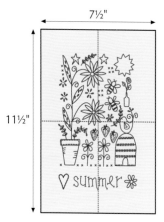

Embroidery placement

4. Layer the embroidered rectangle, batting, and backing; baste. Using fabric that matches the embroidery, make single-fold binding (see page 63); attach it to the quilt.

✕ MAKING THE QUILT ✕

Use a ¼" seam allowance and press as indicated by the arrows on the diagrams. For information on any of the quilting or finishing steps, go to ShopMartingale.com/HowtoQuilt for downloadable information.

1. Sew strip A to the right side of the cream center rectangle.

2. Working in a counterclockwise direction, sew the 2½" strips to the embroidery in alphabetical order.

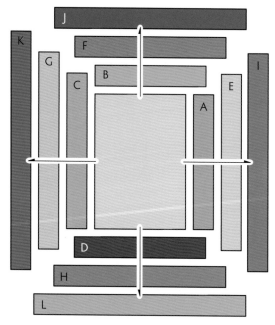

Make 1 block,
21½" × 25½".

3. Layer the quilt top, batting, and backing; baste.

4. Machine quilt a meander design in the cream center. Use the ecru pearl cotton and big-stitch quilting (see page 62) to hand quilt ¼" inside the long edge of each border strip, *except* at the outer edges of strips I–L. (You'll quilt around the perimeter after attaching the binding in step 6.) Trim the batting and backing even with the quilt top.

5. To make an optional hanging sleeve and attach it prior to binding, fold the short ends of a 5" × 18" strip of fabric under ¼" twice and topstitch to hem. Fold the strip in half lengthwise, *wrong* sides together, and press. Aligning the raw edges, stitch the folded strip to the top of the wall hanging back, ⅛" from the raw edge.

6. Using the navy 2½" strips, make and attach double-fold binding (see page 63).

7. Using the ecru pearl cotton, quilt ¼" from the binding seam, along the long edges *only* of strips I–L, folding the hanging sleeve out of the way if you added one. Stitch the lower edge of the sleeve to the backing by hand.

8. Measure 1½" down and in from the top-left corner of the cream center rectangle and mark this point using the Pigma pen. Center the bar portion of a skirt hook-and-eye set horizontally over the mark. Hand sew in place. Repeat for the other side, centering the bar 1½" down and in from the top-right corner.

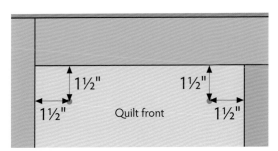

Mark.

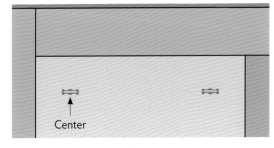

Bar placement

9. Sew two skirt hooks onto the back of each embroidery, placing each hook ⅜" from the upper binding seam and centered 1½" from the side binding seam. Attach the embroidery to the background and change as desired.

Skirt hooks make it easy to swap embroideries.

× HANGING OPTION ×

As an alternative to using skirt hook-and-eye sets to attach the embroideries, you could instead use Velcro. Sew the hook part to the quilt. Then sew the loop part to the back of the embroidery to correspond with the hook placement. You'll need to attach pieces of loop tape to each of the interchangeable panels, but the panels are small enough that just 1" at each end will support their weight.

Spring panel

Winter panel

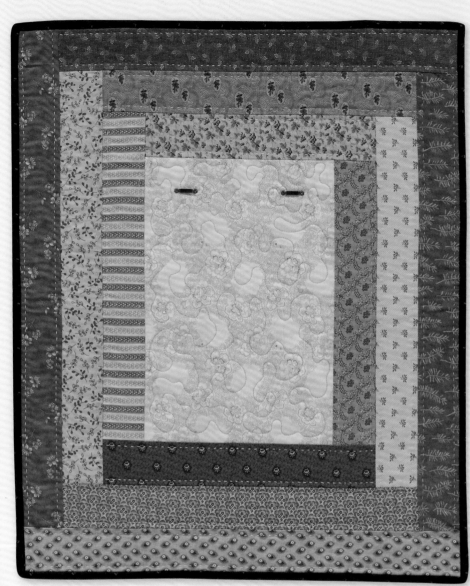

Finished quilt: 21½" × 25½"
Finished embroidery panels:
7½" × 11½"

Fill in with
backstitch.

Satin stitch

Embroidery Key

——— Backstitch

▰▰▰ Chain stitch

✕ Cross-stitch

• French knot

◠ Lazy daisy

– – – Running stitch

▆▆ Satin stitch

♥ spring

Fill in with backstitch.

Satin stitch

♥ summer ✳

Satin stitch

Embroidery Key

——— Backstitch

▬▬▬ Chain stitch

✕ Cross-stitch

• French knot

◯ Lazy daisy

– – – Running stitch

■ Satin stitch

autumn

Embroidery Key

———	Backstitch
▬▬▬▬	Chain stitch
✕	Cross-stitch
•	French knot
◡	Lazy daisy
– – –	Running stitch

Our Home

To change the sentiment around your home with sweet verses, display this little wall hanging where family and guests alike will enjoy your home-sweet-home stitchery.

× MATERIALS ×

Supplies are for one background quilt and three interchangeable embroidered panels. Yardage is based on 42"-wide fabric. Fat eighths are 9" × 21".

QUILT
1 fat eighth of blue floral for sky
1 rectangle, 6½" × 8½", of tan floral for quilt center
¼ yard of teal floral for outer border
⅓ yard of navy print for binding
1 rectangle, 3½" × 9", of red dot for house roof
9 pairs of assorted print squares, 2½" × 2½"
  (18 total), for inner border
1 rectangle, 21" × 28", of backing fabric
1 rectangle, 21" × 28", of batting
30" length of cream lace, ¾" wide
4 sets of snap fasteners, ¾" diameter
Ecru pearl cotton, size 8, for hand quilting
Pigma pen
¼" quilter's tape (optional; see page 62)

EMBROIDERIES
4 rectangles, 8" × 10", of cream print for
  backgrounds
4 rectangles, 8" × 10", of lightweight fusible
  interfacing for backing
3 assorted strips, 1½" × 42", for binding
3 rectangles, 6½" × 8½", of backing fabric
3 rectangles, 6½" × 8½", of batting
6-strand embroidery floss in red, purple, dark
  pink, variegated light green, dark green,
  medium blue, gold, and brown

× CUTTING ×

From the blue floral, cut:
- 1 strip, 3½" × 21"; crosscut into 2 rectangles, 3½" × 5¼"
- 1 strip, 2½" × 21"; crosscut into 2 rectangles, 2½" × 5½"
- 1 strip, 1½" × 12½"

From the teal floral, cut:
- 2 strips, 2½" × 42"; crosscut into:
    2 strips, 2½" × 19½"
    2 strips, 2½" × 16½"

From the navy print, cut:
- 3 strips, 2½" × 42"

✕ EMBROIDERING THE DESIGNS ✕

1. Press the cream rectangles. Trace each embroidery design (pages 24–27) onto the right side of a rectangle. Fuse the interfacing to the backs of the marked rectangles.

2. Using two strands of floss, embroider each verse following the embroidery keys on the patterns.

3. Trim the three verse pieces to 6½" × 8½". Trim the embroidered house piece to 5½" × 8½".

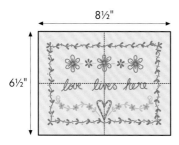

Embroidery placement

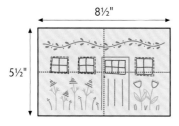

Embroidery placement

✕ FINISHING THE EMBROIDERED VERSES ✕

1. Cut the lace into two 6½" lengths and two 8½" lengths. Place the lace around the raw edges of the Home Sweet Home embroidery; baste.

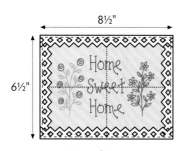

Lace placement

2. Layer each embroidered piece with batting and backing; baste. Use a 1½" strip to make and attach single-fold binding (see page 63) to each.

✕ MAKING THE QUILT ✕

Use a ¼" seam allowance and press as indicated by the arrows on the diagrams. For information on any of the quilting or finishing steps, go to ShopMartingale.com/HowtoQuilt for downloadable information.

1. Sew a blue 2½" × 5½" rectangle to each side of the embroidered house rectangle to make a unit measuring 5½" × 12½", including seam allowances.

Make 1 unit,
5½" × 12½".

2. Referring to the diagram below, lay the blue 3½" × 5¼" rectangles on the red rectangle, right sides together. On the blue rectangles, mark diagonal lines from the upper inner corner to the red rectangle's lower corner. Sew on the lines. Trim the triangles and fold the blue rectangles back to make a roof unit measuring 3½" × 12½", including seam allowances.

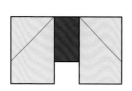

Make 1 unit,
3½" × 12½".

Finished quilt: 16½" × 23½"

Finished embroidery panels: 6½" × 8½"

Make this sweet wall hanging as a housewarming gift for a dear friend in a new home.

4. Sew the roof unit to the top of the house unit. Sew the 1½" × 12½" blue floral strip to the top of the roof to make a house block measuring 9½" × 12½", including seam allowances.

Make 1 house block,
9½" × 12½".

5. Arrange the 18 assorted 2½" squares around the tan rectangle. Sew two sets of three squares for the side borders. Sew two sets of six squares for the top and bottom borders.

Make 2 side borders,
2½" × 6½".

Make 2 top/bottom borders,
2½" × 12½".

6. Sew the side borders to the sides of the tan rectangle. Add the top and bottom borders to make a patchwork block measuring 10½" × 12½", including seam allowances.

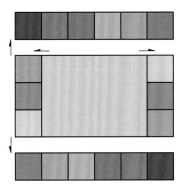

Make 1 patchwork block,
10½" × 12½".

7. Sew the house block to the top of the patchwork block to make a quilt center that measures 12½" × 19½", including seam allowances.

8. Sew the teal 2½" × 19½" strips to the sides of the quilt center. Sew the teal 2½" × 16½" strips to top and bottom.

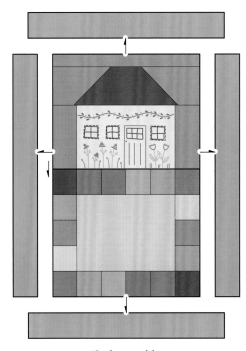

Quilt assembly

9. Layer the pieced top, batting, and backing; baste. Using the ecru pearl cotton, quilter's tape, and big-stitch quilting (see page 62), quilt ¼" from the house and outer edges of the blue background. Quilt ¼" from the interior edge only of the teal border. Quilt diagonal lines from corner to corner in each border square. Quilt wavy lines on the roof.

Quilt diagonal lines in the border squares.

Welcome Friends panel

10. Trim the batting and backing even with the quilt top. Using the navy 2½" strips, make and attach double-fold binding (see page 63). Using ecru pearl cotton, quilt ¼" from binding seam.

11. On the tan rectangle, measure ½" from the top and sides at each top corner. Use the Pigma pen to make a mark; sew the stud piece from a snap fastener to one corner and the socket piece to the other, centering each over a mark, as shown at right.

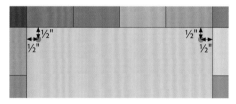

Mark.

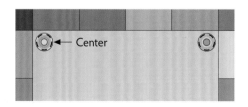

Snap placement

Home Sweet Home panel

12. Repeat for the top back of each embroidered verse, measuring in ¾" from each side and top. Be sure to sew the correct pieces to each corner so that you can snap the embroideries onto the quilt.

Mark.

13. Attach an embroidered rectangle to the snap fasteners on the quilt. Change as desired.

Snap fasteners keep panels securely attached.

Satin stitch → ●

Embroidery Key

───── Backstitch

✕ Cross-stitch

● French knot

◯ Lazy daisy

– – – Running stitch

■ Satin stitch

Home Sweet Home

Satin stitch

Fill in with French knots.

love lives here

Embroidery Key

——— Backstitch

✕ Cross-stitch

• French knot

◯ Lazy daisy

– – – Running stitch

Celebration Banners

Hang these banners to celebrate wonderful holidays
and special occasions throughout the year.

× MATERIALS FOR ONE BANNER ×

1 rectangle, 7" × 11", of cream print
1 rectangle, 7" × 11", of lightweight fusible
    interfacing
Ecru pearl cotton, size 8, for hand quilting
¼"-wide quilter's tape (optional; see page 62)
Optional: metal quilt hanger (Ackfeldwire.com)

EASTER
1 strip, 1½" × 42", of light blue print for border
1 strip, 1½" × 42", of red print for binding
1 rectangle, 12" × 20", of fabric for backing
    and sleeve
1 rectangle, 12" × 17", of batting
6-strand embroidery floss in dark red, light blue,
    navy, brown, orange, yellow, pink, light green,
    medium green, and variegated dark green
40" length of cream lace, ⅝" wide

HALLOWEEN
1 strip, 1½" × 42", of black print for border
1 strip, 1½" × 42", of black print for binding
1 rectangle, 12" × 20", of fabric for backing
    and sleeve
1 rectangle, 12" × 17", of batting
6-strand embroidery floss in variegated gray/black
40" length of gray rickrack, ⅝" wide

THANKSGIVING
1 strip, 1½" × 42", of gray print for border
1 strip, 1½" × 42", of rust print for binding
1 rectangle, 12" × 20", of fabric for backing
    and sleeve
1 rectangle, 12" × 17", of batting
6-strand embroidery floss in variegated
    red/gray/tan

CHRISTMAS
1 strip, 1½" × 42", of holly print for border
1 strip, 1½" × 42", of green print for binding
1 rectangle, 12" × 20", of fabric for backing
    and sleeve
1 rectangle, 12" × 17", of batting
6-strand embroidery floss in variegated red

BIRTHDAY
¼ yard of red floral for border
⅛ yard of navy print for binding
1 rectangle, 14" × 22", of fabric for backing
    and sleeve
1 rectangle, 14" × 19", of batting
6-strand embroidery floss in dark red, variegated
    yellow, variegated navy, and variegated green
7" length of red rickrack, ½" wide
50" length of cream rickrack, ½" wide

WHAT MAKES YOU HAPPY
¼ yard of blue floral for border
⅛ yard of navy print for binding
1 rectangle, 14" × 22", of fabric for backing
    and sleeve
1 rectangle, 14" × 19", of batting
6-strand embroidery floss in dark red, variegated
    pink, yellow, brown, variegated navy, and
    variegated green

VALENTINE
¼ yard of pink print for border
⅛ yard of pink print for binding
1 rectangle, 14" × 22", of fabric for backing
    and sleeve
1 rectangle, 14" × 19", of batting
6-strand embroidery floss in variegated pink/beige

⋈ CUTTING ⋈

From the Easter, Halloween, Thanksgiving, or Christmas border fabric, cut:
- 3 strips, 1½" × 7½"
- 1 strip, 1½" × 8½"
- 1 strip, 1½" × 6½"

From the ¼-yard Birthday, What Makes You Happy, or Valentine border fabric, cut:
- 2 strips, 2½" × 42"; crosscut into:
  - 3 rectangles, 2½" × 7½"
  - 1 rectangle, 2½" × 10½"
  - 1 rectangle, 2½" × 9¾"

From the ⅛-yard Birthday, What Makes You Happy, or Valentine binding fabric, cut:
- 2 strips, 1½" × 42"

⋈ EMBROIDERING THE DESIGN ⋈

1. Press the cream rectangles. Trace one of the patterns on pages 40–46 and the banner outline onto the right side of a rectangle, extending the upper edge ½" above the dashed line. Fuse the interfacing rectangle to the back of the marked rectangle. The banner outline will be the cutting line.

2. Using two strands of floss, embroider the design following the embroidery key on the pattern.

3. Trim the embroidered piece on the banner outline.

Embroidery placement   Trim.

⋈ ASSEMBLING THE BANNERS ⋈

Use a ¼" seam allowance and press as indicated by the arrows on the diagrams.

EASTER, HALLOWEEN, THANKSGIVING, AND CHRISTMAS BANNERS

1. Sew 1½" × 7½" strips to the left and right sides of the embroidered piece. Sew the 1½" × 8½" strip to the top. Sew the 1½" × 6½" strip to the right diagonal side and the 1½" × 7½" strip to the left diagonal side. Use a rotary cutter and ruler to trim, aligning the ruler with the outer side and diagonal edges.

Trim.

Trim. →

2. Layer the embroidered banner top, batting, and backing; baste. On the Thanksgiving banner, use ecru pearl cotton and big-stitch quilting (see page 62) to stitch wavy lines in the middle of the border. On the Christmas banner, make straight stitches in the border, ¼" from the seam.

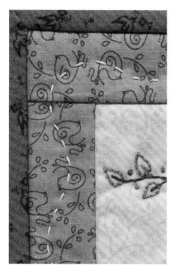

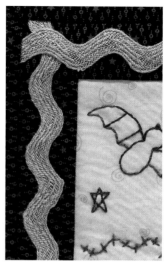

Quilt curves on the Thanksgiving banner.

Quilt a straight line on the Christmas banner.

Embellish the Easter banner with lace.

Stitch rickrack onto the Halloween banner.

3. On the Easter banner, place lace trim ⅛" from the raw edges, with the scallops facing inward, and baste in place. On the Halloween banner, place a 14½" length of rickrack centered along each side of the border and around the angle, overlapping at the bottom point, and then stitch it in place. Stitch a 9" length of rickrack across the top.

BIRTHDAY, WHAT MAKES YOU HAPPY, AND VALENTINE BANNERS

1. Baste the red rickrack along the top of the Birthday banner and stitch in place with pearl cotton, using French knots.

Easter banner lace placement

Halloween banner rickrack placement

2. Sew 2½" × 7½" rectangles to the left and right sides. Sew the 2½" × 10½" rectangle to the top. Sew a 2½" × 7½" rectangle to the right diagonal side. Sew the 2½" × 9¾" rectangle to the left diagonal side. Use a rotary cutter and ruler to trim, aligning the ruler with the outer side and diagonal edges.

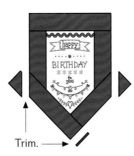

On the What Makes You Happy banner, quilt ¼" from the inner and outer edges.

3. Layer the banner, batting, and backing; baste. On the Birthday and What Makes You Happy banners, use ecru pearl cotton, quilter's tape, and big-stitch quilting (see page 62) to quilt ¼" from the inner edge only of the border. On the Valentine banner, quilt a wavy line across each border strip.

Quilt wavy lines in the border of the Valentine banner.

Birthday banner

4. For the Birthday banner, align the cream rickrack with the raw edges. Baste in place.

Align with
raw edge.

Birthday banner
rickrack placement

Maintaining an accurate ¼"-wide seam allowance when attaching the binding ensures that the rickrack's scallops will be a consistent depth.

✕ FINISHING ✕

For information on any of the quilting or finishing steps, go to ShopMartingale.com/HowtoQuilt for downloadable information.

1. Trim the batting and backing even with the quilt top. Use the 1½"-wide strips to make and attach single-fold binding (see page 63). Sew the binding to the front only; do not stitch it to the back yet.

2. From the fabric for the backing and sleeve, cut a strip 3" wide by the width of the banner less 4". Fold the strip in half, wrong sides together and with long edges aligned; sew ¼" from each short end. Turn right side out and press. Align the raw edge of the sleeve with the top raw edge of the banner. Baste in place. Sew the folded edge to the back of the quilt, leaving the short ends open.

Be careful not to stitch through to the front of the banner when sewing the sleeve's folded edge to the backing.

3. Hand stitch the binding to the back of the banner. On the What Makes You Happy banner, use the ecru pearl cotton to quilt ¼" from the binding seam.

Finished sizes:
Large: 10½" × 15½"
Small: 8½" × 13"

Changing Seasons

Surprise a special friend
or relative with
the gift of an
embroidered banner.

Valentine's Day banner

Easter banner

DO MORE
of
what
makes you
HAPPY

happy

EASTER

Embroidery Key

—— Backstitch

✕ Cross-stitch

• French knot

◠ Lazy daisy

- - - Running stitch

■ Satin stitch

Satin stitch

happy

HALLOWEEN

When tracing onto background, mark upper edge ½" above dashed line.

Embroidery Key

——— Backstitch

⊤⊤⊤⊤⊤ Blanket stitch

✕ Cross-stitch

• French knot

⌒ Lazy daisy

- - - Running stitch

■ Satin stitch

Fill in with backstitch.

Satin stitch

Fill in with French knots.

Embroidery Key

——— Backstitch

▬▬▬▬ Chain stitch

• French knot

⟲ Lazy daisy

- - - - Running stitch

Embroidery Key

——— Backstitch

✕ Cross-stitch

• French knot

◯ Lazy daisy

- - - Running stitch

Words of Wisdom

*Display colorful words of wisdom
to inspire you every day.*

× MATERIALS ×

*Supplies are for 1 framed background and
3 interchangeable embroidered blocks. Yardage is
based on 42"-wide fabric. Fat quarters are 18" × 21".
Fat eighths are 9" × 21".*

⅓ yard of cream print for embroidery backgrounds
1 fat quarter of blue floral for frame background
3 squares, 10" × 10", of lightweight fusible
    interfacing for embroidery backing
3 fat quarters of backing fabric for embroidered
    blocks
3 squares, 16" × 16", of batting for embroidered
    blocks
1 square, 21" × 21", of batting for framed
    background
6-strand embroidery floss in red, pink, light green,
    variegated green, dark green, brown, light blue,
    navy, purple, and yellow
Ecru pearl cotton, size 8, for quilting
4 sets of Velcro hook-and-loop circles, ⅞" diameter
Wooden frame with 16" × 16" opening
Erasable pen or pencil for dark fabric
Basting spray
¼" quilter's tape (optional; see page 62)

LIFE IS BETTER
1 fat eighth of light blue check for border
1 strip, 2½" × 21", of navy print for border
⅛ yard of navy tone on tone for binding

BRING JOY
¼ yard of red floral for border and binding
⅛ yard of olive print for border

GIVE THANKS
⅛ yard of purple print for border
2½" × 11" strip of green print for border
⅛ yard of brown stripe for binding

× CUTTING ×

From the cream print, cut:
- 3 squares, 10" × 10"

From the blue floral, cut:
- 1 square, 17" × 17"

LIFE IS BETTER BLOCK

Inspire grins by displaying this charming block where folks can see it up close.

✕ CUTTING ✕

From the light blue check, cut:
- 3 strips, 2½" × 21"; crosscut into:
  4 rectangles, 2½" × 8½"
  4 squares, 2½" × 2½"

From the navy print, cut:
- 8 squares, 2½" × 2½"

From the navy tone on tone, cut:
- 2 strips, 1½" × 42"

✕ EMBROIDERING THE DESIGN ✕

1. Press a cream square. Trace the Life Is Better design (page 57) onto the right side of the square. Fuse an interfacing square to the wrong side of the marked square.

2. Using two strands of floss, embroider the design following the embroidery key and colors shown on the pattern.

✕ ASSEMBLING THE QUILT ✕

Use a ¼" seam allowance and press as indicated by the arrows on the diagrams.

1. Centering the embroidery, trim the stitched square to 8½" × 8½".

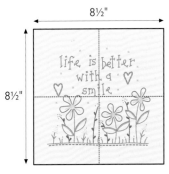

Embroidery placement

2. Draw a diagonal line from corner to corner on the back of the navy squares. Place a marked square, right sides together, on each end of one of the light blue rectangles. Sew on the lines and trim the excess. Fold the navy fabric over. Make four units.

Make 4 units,
2½" × 8½".

3. Sew light blue units to the sides of the embroidered square, noting the direction of the blue triangle ends as shown in the photo above.

Your local thrift store or antique shop is a fun place to look for frames.

Finished framed background: 16" × 16"

4. Sew a light blue square to each end of the remaining units. Sew one to the top of the embroidered piece and one to the bottom, again noting the direction of the triangles.

Make 1 block,
12½" × 12½".

× QUILTING AND FINISHING ×

For information on any of the quilting or finishing steps, go to ShopMartingale.com/HowtoQuilt for downloadable information.

1. Layer the block, batting, and backing; baste. Using pearl cotton, quilter's tape, and big-stitch quilting (see page 62), quilt ¼" inside the center square and ¼" inside each navy triangle, using the quilter's tape as a guide, if desired.

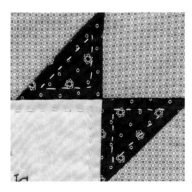

2. Trim the batting and backing even with the block.

3. Using the navy 1½" strips, make single-fold binding (see page 63); attach it to the quilt.

BRING JOY BLOCK

Take pleasure in everyday things with this embroidered reminder.

× CUTTING ×

From the red floral, cut:
- 1 strip, 3" × 42"; crosscut into 2 squares, 3" × 3"
- Cut the remainder of the 3" strip into 2 strips, 1½" × 36"; crosscut into 4 rectangles, 1½" × 8½"
- 2 strips, 1½" × 42"

From the olive print, cut:
- 1 strip, 3" × 42"; crosscut into 2 squares, 3" × 3"
- Cut the remainder of the 3" strip into 2 strips, 1½" × 36"; crosscut into 4 rectangles, 1½" × 8½"

× EMBROIDERING THE DESIGN ×

1. Press a cream square. Trace the Bring Joy design (page 58) onto the right side of the square. Fuse an interfacing square to the wrong side of the marked square.

2. Using two strands of floss, embroider the design following the embroidery key and colors shown on the pattern.

× ASSEMBLING THE QUILT ×

Use a ¼" seam allowance and press as indicated by the arrows on the diagrams.

1. Centering the embroidery, trim the stitched square to 8½" × 8½".

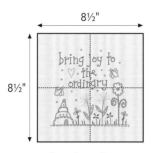

Embroidery placement

2. Draw a diagonal line from corner to corner on the back of the red floral squares. Place a marked square, right sides together, on each of the olive squares. Stitch ¼" from each side of the marked line. Cut on the drawn line and press to make four half-square-triangle units. Trim each unit to 2½" square.

Make 4 units.

3. Sew red and olive rectangles together along their length to make a strip unit. Make four. Sew two half-square-triangle units to each end of the remaining two strip units, noting the direction of the triangles.

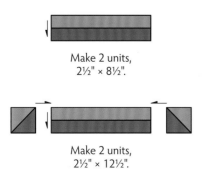

Make 2 units, 2½" × 8½".

Make 2 units, 2½" × 12½".

4. Sew strip units to the sides of the embroidered square, with the red fabric next to the square. Sew a half-square-triangle strip unit to the top of the embroidered piece and one to the bottom, again noting the direction of the triangles.

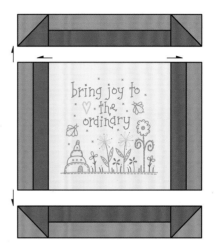

Make 1 block, 12½" × 12½".

× QUILTING AND FINISHING ×

For information on any of the quilting or finishing steps, go to ShopMartingale.com/HowtoQuilt for downloadable information.

1. Layer the block, batting, and backing; baste. Using pearl cotton and big-stitch quilting (see page 62), quilt ¼" inside the center square and ¼" inside the red patches, using the quilter's tape as a guide.

2. Trim batting and backing even with quilt top.

3. Using the red 1½" strips, make single-fold binding; attach it to the quilt.

GIVE THANKS BLOCK

Place this design where you'll see it every day, as you're sure to feel gratitude whenever you spy this sweet block.

✕ CUTTING ✕

From the purple print, cut:
- 1 strip, 2½" × 42"; crosscut into 4 rectangles, 2½" × 8½"

From the green print, cut:
- 4 squares, 2½" × 2½"

From the brown stripe, cut:
- 2 strips, 1½" × 42"

✕ EMBROIDERING THE DESIGN ✕

1. Press a cream square. Trace the Give Thanks design (page 59) onto the right side of the square. Fuse an interfacing square to the wrong side of the marked square.

2. Using two strands of floss, embroider the design following the embroidery key and colors shown on the pattern.

✕ ASSEMBLING THE QUILT ✕

Use a ¼" seam allowance and press as indicated by the arrows on the diagrams.

1. Centering the embroidery, trim the stitched square to 8½" × 8½".

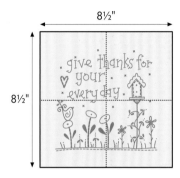

Embroidery placement

2. Sew a purple rectangle to the left and right sides of the embroidered square. Sew a green square to each end of the remaining purple rectangles. Sew one green-and-purple strip to the top of the embroidered piece and one to the bottom.

Make 1 block,
12½" × 12½".

× QUILTING AND FINISHING ×

For information on any of the quilting or finishing steps, go to ShopMartingale.com/HowtoQuilt for downloadable information.

1. Layer the wall-hanging top, batting, and backing; baste. Using pearl cotton and big-stitch quilting (see page 62), quilt ¼" inside the center square, a wavy line in the purple borders, and a cross in each green corner square, using the quilter's tape as a guide, if desired.

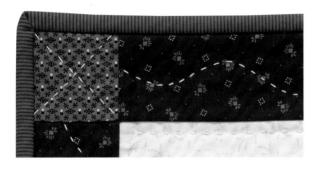

2. Trim the batting and backing even with the top.

3. Using the brown stripe 1½" strips, make single-fold binding; attach it to the quilt.

× ASSEMBLY AND FRAMING ×

1. Centering it 2½" from the edges, draw a 12" square in the middle of the blue floral backing square using an erasable pen or pencil. Layer the batting behind the square and use big-stitch quilting (see page 62) to quilt a wavy line in the border area (outside the marked square) with ecru pearl cotton.

2. At each of the upper corners of the blue square, center a Velcro circle 2⅝" from the edges, placing a hook circle at one corner and a loop circle at the other. Sew to secure. Lightly place the opposite Velcro circle (loop on hook and hook on loop) on each sewn circle, then lay a finished block on top. Holding the unsecured circles in place, flip the block over and stitch the circles in place. (The circles should be centered 1⅛" from the block edges.) Repeat for all blocks.

Velcro dots make it easy to swap blocks and don't add bulk.

3. Trim the blue square to the size of the frame's backing board. Lightly spray the board with basting spray. Attach the blue square to the board and place inside the frame.

4. Attach one of the embroidered pieces to the framed background.

× USING VELCRO EFFICIENTLY ×

Separate the pieces of a single hook-and-loop set and sew one of each type to the background. Repeat for each embroidery, using one hook and one loop piece per block. Make sure that hook pieces face loop pieces. This will use the sets efficiently, and you won't have to worry about having only hook pieces or loop pieces left over.

Satin stitch

Embroidery Key

─── Backstitch	⬯ Lazy daisy
⊤⊤⊤⊤⊤ Blanket stitch	─ ─ ─ Running stitch
●━━● Chain stitch	■ Satin stitch
✕ Cross-stitch	·········· Stem stitch
• French knot	

bring joy to
♡ the
ordinary

Fill in with
backstitch.

Fill in with
backstitch.

Satin stitch.

Fill in with
French knots.

Fill in with
French
knots.

give thanks for
your
every day

Satin stitch.

Fill in with
backstitch.

Satin stitch.

Satin stitch.

Fill in with
backstitch.

Satin stitch.

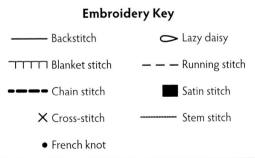

Embroidery Key

——	Backstitch	⬯	Lazy daisy
⊤⊤⊤⊤⊤	Blanket stitch	– – –	Running stitch
▬▬▬	Chain stitch	■	Satin stitch
✕	Cross-stitch	········	Stem stitch
●	French knot		

GENERAL INSTRUCTIONS

The projects in this book combine my love of hand embroidery with machine piecing and hand quilting. I'll review some of the basic information you'll need, but if you're new to sewing and quilting, you can find additional helpful information at ShopMartingale.com/HowtoQuilt, where you can download free illustrated how-to guides on everything from rotary cutting to binding a quilt.

✕ EMBROIDERY INSTRUCTIONS ✕

Here you'll find a list of the embroidery tools and techniques I like best. However, there are many different styles and techniques, so try different methods to find the stitches, threads, fabrics, and techniques that work well for you and that you enjoy the most.

NEEDLES

Hand-sewing needles come in packages labeled by type and size. The larger the needle size, the smaller the needle (a size 1 needle will be longer and thicker than a size 12 needle). For embroidery, I like to use a size 8 embroidery needle, also referred to as a crewel needle. An embroidery needle is similar to a Sharp, but with an elongated eye designed to accommodate six-strand floss or pearl cotton. You may prefer a size 7 or 9. For appliqué, I use a size 10 straw needle, also called a milliner's or appliqué needle, but a size 9 or 11 may be your preference. When hand quilting with size 8 pearl cotton, I prefer to use a size 5 or 6 embroidery needle. This allows me to thread the needle easily. Test a few needles until you find one that suits you; any brand is fine.

THREADS

I like to use a variety of threads. Some threads I select to match the fabrics I plan to use; sometimes I pick a thread first and then choose appropriate fabrics. Six-strand embroidery floss is the most common floss used. It needs to be split before stitching since only two or three strands are used at once. I prefer to use two strands and have used two strands for most of the projects in this book. Some threads, such as the pearl cotton I use when quilting, can be used straight off the spool or ball. I always knot my threads when embroidering.

Because I back the embroidered squares with fusible interfacing before stitching, I don't need to worry that the knots are going to show through. To begin embroidering, thread your needle with the chosen floss and make a knot at the end of the strand. When you have 4" to 5" of floss left, or when you've completed the stitching, insert the needle so that it's on the back of the embroidery. Then, loop the thread around the needle and push the resulting knot close to the back of the stitch you've just finished.

My favorite threads for embroidery are Aurifil Mako Cotton 12-weight thread; 6-strand embroidery floss from Cottage Garden Threads, DMC, and Weeks Dye Works; the Gentle Art sampler threads; and size 12 pearl cotton from DMC or Valdani. My favorite thread for quilting is DMC size 8 pearl cotton. I've used all of these threads in the projects in this book.

TRACING THE DESIGN

To trace or transfer the embroidery design onto your fabric, I recommend using a light box. Tape the design in place on the light box, and then center the fabric on top of the design and secure it in place. Use a brown fine-point Pigma pen to trace lightly over the design. A fine-point washable

× EMBROIDERY STITCHES ×

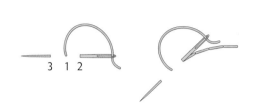

Backstitch

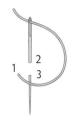

Blanket stitch

Chain stitch

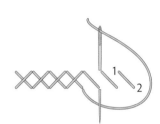

Cross-stitch

French knot

Lazy daisy stitch

Running stitch

Satin stitch

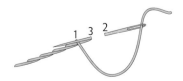

Stem stitch

marker, a ceramic pencil (such as Sewline), or a mechanical or wooden pencil with a fine, hard lead will also work.

If you don't have a light box, tape the design to a window or use a glass-topped table with a lamp underneath. I always trace the minimum. For instance, when tracing lazy daisy stitches (loops on the embroidery pattern), I only mark a dot where I will start the stitch. I typically don't trace dotted lines for running stitches; I stitch them by referring to the pattern illustration or photo. Trace only the straight line for blanket stitching. You'll soon find the sort of marking that will work best for you.

EMBROIDERY FABRIC AND INTERFACING

For easier tracing, choose a light-colored fabric for the background. It's fine to use a subtle print, such as a small polka dot; the print will add some interest. Tone-on-tone fabrics are also nice to use. Some patterns call for linen. This should be a very lightweight, finely woven linen.

I always back my traced fabric with a very lightweight fusible interfacing. This prevents show-through of the embroidery threads and knots. And, because the interfacing stiffens the fabric a bit, there is less distortion of the fabric and stitches when the embroidered piece is hooped. To do this, cut a piece of interfacing the same size and shape as your background fabric and, following the manufacturer's instructions, fuse it in place *after* tracing the design and *before* stitching.

HOOPS

I use an embroidery hoop to keep the fabric taut, but not tight, while stitching. Hoops are available in wood, metal, and plastic, with different mechanisms for keeping the fabric taut. Any type of hoop is fine; just take the time to find one you're comfortable with. A 4" hoop is my preferred size, but you may prefer a 5" or 6" hoop. Remember to always remove your fabric from the hoop when you've finished stitching for the day.

× SEWING AND QUILTING INSTRUCTIONS ×

Please read through the instructions carefully before starting. For all projects, the yardage is based on 42"-wide fabric and the seam allowances are always ¼". I press the seam allowances away from the embroidered fabric and toward the darker fabrics whenever possible.

BATTING

I like to use cotton batting in all my quilts. It's fairly thin and easy to work with. It also handles well and feels nice.

BIG-STITCH QUILTING

To add a little dimension to my projects, I hand quilt them using big-stitch quilting and size 8 ecru pearl cotton. I begin by placing ¼" quilter's tape so that one side adjoins a seamline or other feature of my project, such as an embroidered circle. Using the edge of the quilter's tape as a guide allows me to stitch a quilting line that is even and exactly ¼" from the seam. Quilter's tape comes on a roll and is both inexpensive and repositionable.

Thread your needle with pearl cotton thread, inserting the end straight off the ball. Cut a length of thread about 15" long. Knot one end with a single knot. Insert your needle through the backing fabric to the front, where you want to start. Pull the backing fabric away from the batting and pull on the thread. Tug gently so the knot pops into the layers. Bring the needle up through the quilt top right next to the ¼" quilter's tape, and then insert it back into the quilt right next to the tape and approximately ¼" from the spot where your needle came up. This will make a "big stitch" approximately ¼" long. Bring the needle back up next to the quilter's tape, ¼" from the point where the needle went down last. Continue in this manner until you have 4" to 5" of thread left. Take the thread to the back, knot it, and then pull the knot back into the quilt, between the backing and the batting. Bring the needle out approximately 1" away. Trim the thread close to the backing fabric. For "wavy" line quilting, freehand the quilting as you stitch.

DOUBLE-FOLD BINDING

For big quilts and larger wall hangings, I use 2½"-wide fabric strips to make double-fold binding. Cut the number of strips listed in the project, and then sew them together end to end. Press the seam allowances open. Fold over one end of the strip at a 45° angle to form the start, and then fold the strip in half lengthwise, wrong sides together.

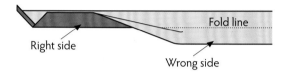

Place the starting end of the binding on the front of the quilt, at least 8" from a corner, and with the raw edges of the quilt and the folded strip aligned. Begin to sew the binding to the quilt a few inches from the folded end of the binding. Continue to stitch the binding to the quilt, mitering the corners as you go. When you're a few inches from the start, trim the end of your strip to the length needed to tuck it into the folded end at the beginning. Fold the beginning end of the strip over the tucked-in end, and aligning raw edges, sew the last few inches of the binding to the quilt. Fold the binding over to the back and slip-stitch it in place.

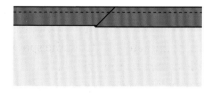

SINGLE-FOLD BINDING

For smaller projects, such as the banners and all the mini-quilts, a wide, double-fold binding is too bulky, so I use a single-fold binding instead. For single-fold binding, cut fabric strips 1½" wide. Stitch the strips together and press the seam allowances open as for 2½"-wide binding. Press under ¼" along one long edge to form a fold. (This edge will be turned to the back of the project and sewn in place once the binding is attached to the front.) Fold over ¼" at one end. Sew the raw edge of the binding to the project as for double-fold binding. When you get back to the beginning, trim the binding strip so that it overlaps the folded start by ¼" to ½". Continue sewing over the lapped binding until you've reached the stitching at the beginning. Fold the binding to the back of the project and slip-stitch the pressed edge of the binding in place. Hold with binder clips or pins while you slip-stitch the binding in place.

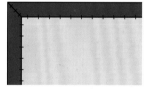

Meet the Author

Gail Pan

I live on the outskirts of Melbourne, at the foot of the beautiful Dandenong Ranges (a series of low, verdant mountain ranges). Growing up in a home where sewing was always an important part of life, it was only natural that I tried every craft there was! I have always had some kind of project in the works, from knitting to cross-stitch.

When my kids were little, I made their clothes, and when they got too old for that, I moved to patchwork. My design business was born out of a habit of always changing whatever I was working on until it became a new design. In 2003, some friends who were opening their own patchwork business encouraged me to design and release my own patterns. I have been designing ever since. I have also branched out into designing fabric, which is so much fun!

I teach all over the world and get great satisfaction and enjoyment from sharing my love of needle and thread. I have met some amazing women whom I now call friends. I hope to count you among them. Happy stitching!